# A BOOK FOR THE SHELF

## RANTINGS AND WRITINGS OF A BLACK, QUEER, POLYAMOROUS WOMAN

ARIELLE CLARK

NANNY
GOAT
BOOKS

**Nanny Goat Press**
**Louisville, KY**

nannygoat.press

A Book For The Shelf

First Edition.

ISBN: 978-1-954002-00-5

CONTENTS

*To Highland Coffee in Louisville, Kentucky,*
*For letting me sit in your coffee shop and write for hours;*

*To the strong black folks who raised me*
*For teaching me everything I know;*

*To the queer black folks*
*Whose existence is a revolution*
*And Whom I hope I make proud;*

*To the white people,*
*Straight people,*
*Cis men,*
*Monogamous people,*
*And neurotypical people*
*Who said enough dumb shit to me*
*and irritated me enough to write this book;*

*And to Audre Lorde*

*For being my guide and inspiration*
*And for showing me that I, too, can be heard.*
*When I come to meet the ancestors, I'm gonna have lunch*
*with you.*
*Count on it.*

# FOREWORD

From the moment I met Arielle, I knew that she would rise above all the obstacles the world throws at someone who is black/brown, queer, neurodivergent and polyamorous – all the identities that we do not normally see within our community, much less any other. Arielle is a leader and spearhead to a movement unlike any we have seen before: a true visionary with the establishment of the black-owned, woman-owned, LGBTQ-owned (and polyamorous-owned) owned teashop in her home town.

Arielle continues her trailblazing into the world of literature. Through her works, she wraps her care, love, and warmth on you to feel supported and adored. Her words guide you to be open and speak your own truth. Empowered by her truth, you discover your own greatness.

This brilliant piece of work that Arielle has produced is a compilation of poems, stories, and musings for the black and brown bodies who have never felt represented before, the bodies that hold up the strength of ancestors and future generations. This book is a representation of our secrets that are oftentimes withheld and guarded by shadows. This is a glimpse into the exploration of multi- layered identity in its raw, pure, and vulnerable magnificence.

Though the personal narratives of the spectrum of tales of mahogany, cocoa, oak, obsidian, cream and everything in between, we find ourselves in each of the pages.

In this book, you will be taken on a journey through the multi dimensions of the intersectionalities of blackness, queerness, gender identity, polyamory, and sexual prowess.

Fairen Kia

She, Her, Hers
Self-Published Author
CEO, Creator, Founder of Love Thy Belly, LLC

# INTRODUCTION

BY: ARIELLE CLARK

This book has been a long time coming.

To be honest, I got tired of not seeing black, woman, queer authors on the shelves of both local and major bookstores. I would glide in to those bookstores, head held high, watching the white people stare at me as I powerwalked straight to the queer and African-American sections. I would plop my purse down, squat to see the very bottom shelf, and stare at the spines of the books, eyes focused and narrowed. I would pray that I would see some more content, as I had read all the Audre Lorde they had on the shelves. I'll admit that I need to expand my palate; but God, do I love me some Audre. I want to be her when I grow up.

No matter how hopeful I was, the situation was always the same – little to nothing. Little black, woman, queer authors. And polyamory? Neurodivergence? Not a single book with all my identities wrapped in to one.

I wrote this book for visibility. I wrote this book for awareness. I wrote this book so that people like me wouldn't feel so alone.

Lastly, I wrote this book for the those who are still squatting and squinting in front of the bookshelves at those bookstores, looking for a book that speaks to them.

You are not alone. There are millions of us in the world. This book is for you. Stop squatting, love; it's bad for the knees after a while. We ain't Meg Thee Stallion no more. Them knees can't support us droppin' it low like that.

So next time you find a friend kneeling to find a book like this, turn to them, hand them this book, and say, "Here. A book for the shelf."

# MY HISTORY

I am an amalgamation of birthers – the result of millions of contractions, of thousands of cervixes dilating, opening wide, singing, chanting, yelling arias of new life on the West African plain.

I am the product of hundreds of black wombs carrying black babies with ten black fingers and ten black toes and one black struggle. And while our birthers carried us, little did we know that the kicks and jostles we gave our birthers' swollen, stretch-marked stomachs were merely practice for when our black feet would touch the ground and carry the weight of slavery and personhood.

We began to train our legs before we knew what they were, so that we could run to our black siblings, blood and not-blood, for comfort while running for offices and running from our

overbearing parents who are just trying to
protect us from the harsh, harsh world.

The blood in my veins is that of Audre, of Maya, of
Diana and Halle, of Afro-royalty and 4C braids
and plump, pursed lips and wideset hips.

I am the descendant of soulful siblings, of enslaved
people who ran and activists who spoke.

My history is rich, like my ancestors weren't, who
made a dollar out of 15 cents and cuisine out of
inedible scraps slaveowners threw to us,
deeming us unworthy of good meat and
unrestricted freedom.

This is my history. Black is my blood, and rich is the
African soil from whence I came to be.

# DO YOU REMEMBER ME?

## *NAME HAS BEEN CHANGED TO PROTECT IDENTITY*

I smiled politely at the barista taking my order – a kind, soft-spoken white boy who smiled very sweetly as I told him my drink request.

I saw a black barista making my drink. I openly stared at her, and she stared back. I looked back at the barista taking my order, smiled, and handed him my card.

"Arielle...right?" The black barista said to me. I smiled and nodded.

Her eyes lit up, and she grinned. "Do you remember me?"

*Of course I remember you, Mary*.

*I remember seeing you in the hallways of our high school, when I was still vehemently denying my blackness and trying to please white administration and white friends and white strangers. I would see you and think, "She's softspoken and carries herself well. Not like those other black kids. Thank goodness." I was so brainwashed back then.*

*I remember being in drama club together. You would watch me from backstage while I performed. I would watch you, too. I don't think you ever realized. At the time, I didn't know why; but my heart would swell with pride whenever I saw you on that stage. I now know that that's me being proud of a black woman succeeding in a world not made for her.*

*I remember how your hair would be flat-ironed every day and either pulled in to a tight ponytail or hanging freely and framing your angled face. I was so white-washed back then; I thought, "Her hair isn't messy. Good. None of that crazy, nappy, ghetto shit." I was so shitty and judgmental. But now, your hair is in a cute afro, 4C curls bouncing as you work behind the coffee bar. I'm so proud of you for putting down at damn flat iron. Shit fries your ends...believe me. I did it for years.*

*Your smile is so much brighter now. Both you and I have grown so much since those times. We've finally started breaking the chains and shackles of whitewashing. We are finally embracing our melanin, our hair, ourselves, and each other.*

*I remember you. I'm so proud of you. I love you. Keep going. Keep growing. Keep fighting. Keep being beautiful. Keep being fearfully and wonderfully made.*

I smiled and nodded silently. She grinned even harder. "We went to high school together...remember?" I nodded again.

I paid for my drink, sat down, and wrote this chapter while I watched her work.

"Do you remember me?" She asked.

More than you will ever realize, sister. More than you will ever realize.

# MY FIRST TIME HOME

I had become used to foreign lands, to exploring the hills and valleys of bodies with skin starkly brighter than my own. I grew accustomed to the contrast between my sexual partners' skin and my own: brown against the white, coffee blending with sweet cream, the ethereal moon gleaming against the black void of the night sky.

After coupling with each woman, I would lie with her in our post-sex haze, touching one another gently, drawing lazy circles with our fingertips on one another. And as I mindlessly traced crooked shapes against her form, I would quietly observe the dissimilarities of our complexions. At first, I balked; but over time, after many white partners, I fell in to this canyon between us, between our differing tones and experiences.

But then, I went to bed with her.

She hovered over me; and I looked in to her deep, chocolate-brown eyes. She gave me a lopsided smile; and when she spoke, her low, smooth voice warmed the blood pumping through my quivering body. Her bedside lamp poured soft, red light over our bodies. As the glow of the bulb illuminated her skin, I stared intently, taken aback at her beauty.

"You're beautiful," she muttered as she buried her fingers inside of me, pressing her mouth against my neck and her body against my own.

My back arched; and I gasped, gripping her strong, broad shoulders. My eyes widened, and they traveled down her body. Suddenly, the world faded.

Her complexion was like mine – rich, brown, coated in melanin. As my grasp on her shoulders tightened, I admired how our skin seemed to combine. Instead of seeing two shades fighting, competing, refusing to mix like oil and water, they melded together as one, as a single being, as a sole brown entity, a beast of color with two sweating, glistening backs.

Never had I felt so close to anyone. Never had I felt so connected. Through our passionate lovemaking, our black struggles, and our brown existences, our melanin commonalities became one deep, omnipotent being capable of anything and everything.

With a long, high-pitched moan, I gave her my pleasure. I gifted her my orgasm, long and deep, rocking my body to its core. I cried out to our ancestors and descendants, a lion roaring on the African savannah, to announce a beautiful coupling. My nails dug into her sides, and she groaned as the tightness between my legs gripped her fingers and let go, over and over, contracting and pulsing, coating her in my cum.

She withdrew her fingers from me, and I whined quietly at the sudden emptiness. I never wanted her to leave my core, and I never wanted her to leave my side. For what we created together was an African art never seen by anyone, too beautiful to be gazed upon directly.

I crawled up her body, prowling, exploring; and I purred with delight. I burned her with my gaze, and she could feel my power as I channeled our foremothers' pain and labors. I kissed down her stomach; and her body pressed against my warm, full lips. I bit the area below her belly button playfully; and she laughed, a throaty sound from the depths of her heaving chest. I was enamored.

I rose and stared at her breasts. Her dark, erect nipples stood out proudly against her skin; and I admired their color and their size. I had grown so used to quaint, pink nipples that I had grown resentful of my own large, tinted ones. But gazing at hers, so magnificently and defiantly dark and grand, I began to love my own again

I flicked one of her nipples with my warm, wet tongue. Her body seized, and her eyes rolled back. Grinning, I sucked a nipple in to my eager mouth, rolling my tongue over the warm, perky nub, grazing it with my teeth and pulling gently, purring and moaning at the sensation on my lips and tongue. I swore I could taste her ancestral roots.

She squirmed beneath me, putting her hand in my hair. She pressed her pelvis against me and whined impatiently. I could sense how badly she needed me between her legs.

I dipped my head down to her core, and I was taken aback. With her hands in my hair, she pushed her pussy towards my mouth. I held her down by her hips with my hands, purring quietly.

"Not yet, my sweet. Be patient."

I admired the darkness of her vulva and the shade of her pussy. With my fingers, I gently opened her outer lips; and like a flower, she bloomed before me. She was not a white lily with pink inner petals, as to what I was accustomed.

Rather, past her brown outer lips were lighter brown inner lips and a small, swollen clit covered by a shaded hood.

My mouth began to water. I could smell her arousal. Past partners had smelled sweet, light, and flowery; but her scent was strong, heady, and powerful, like the grass of the African plain.

I devoured her with reckless abandon, tasting brown ancestry and rich nectar from African cape daisies. She ground her hips against my face, smearing her mouth-watering ambrosia on my lips and chin. I drank from her well, and I knew from that moment that I could never quench my thirst with honey from white flowers ever again.

I felt her body shake and seize as she released. Her orgasm came quickly, shocking her, taking hold of her body and making her pussy clench and release against my mouth. As her cum poured from her center, I lapped up every drop.

We curled up in one another; and I began to draw slow, lazy circles on her arm. She held me close, and I sighed happily, her head resting against my neck. She closed her eyes and smiled, relaxing in to my touch, her body sinking in to mine.

As I watched my fingers trace along her skin, I smiled to

myself at the lack of contrast. This felt right. This felt good. This felt purposeful, meant to be.

This was my first time home. And I never wanted to leave.

## MY SHIT AIN'T PINK

My shit ain't pink
Like those fucking hats I see
On the blonde heads of white women
Who yell about "pussy power"
But tend to cower
*Any time* you mention that
"not all women have pussies, Karen"
And at this march, wherein
My turf doesn't accept TERFS,
As your ancestors said,
"We don't take kindly to your kind
Around here", Debbie

My shit ain't pink
And what makes you think
That my pussy is lighter
Than this melanin majesty?

'Cause it'd be a fucking travesty
If my vulva weren't as brown

As the skin that you see
And admire in your head
And try to imitate in
Expensive-ass tanning beds

My pussy is brown
And proud
And loud

It is the sweetest fruit
With nectar flowing
Between mahogany petals

And when your tongue touches
That sweet elixir
You can taste
My proud African roots

My shit ain't pink
Matter of fact,
Like Indian ink
She is dark
And strong
Like black coffee
On a cold Monday morning

My shit ain't pink
And don't ever think
That I'm ashamed of the color
Of the African pussy
That lays so beautifully
Between my strong, black girl magic legs

Because I take pride
In my chocolate brown-eyes
And my hips so wide.
Bitch, I'm beauty personified

So once again, Ashley
And Lindsey and Anne
My shit ain't pink
And don't shame me
Because my black pussy
Can steal your man

My shit ain't pink
It's brown and bold
My shit ain't pink
And she's more precious
Than gold

# THE PAIN OF CRITICISM FROM PARENTS OF COLOR

## A TEXT CONVERSATION

Her: "Can you make my mom be nice when she and my dad randomly come for Easter?"

Me: "uhhhhhhhh. I can try?"

Her: "Yeah did I tell you how she wants me to cut out all sugar, alcohol, carbs, & gluten? It will apparently cure all my issues"

Me: "You told me that and I rolled my eyes so damn hard"

Her: "And I know she's gonna say stuff for Easter. 'You know if you did this you would lose weight' 'you know if you did this you would feel a lot better' 'doing this will help your depression' "

Her: "Damn pop culture pseudoscience!"

Her: "And I only have like 32 days to clean my apartment. And she will still find something wrong with it"

Me: "Why are non-white parents always so critical?"

Her: "The sad part? They aren't as harsh as their predecessors"

Her: "Severe critique is part of the inherited pain and inherited oppression from generations before us"

Her: "My mom's aunts used to only take the nieces they liked for stuff and leave the other ones behind. My grandfather told her he wouldn't help her pay for schooling because she was just going to wind up pregnant like her older sister"

Her: "And that's the light side of it unfortunately"

Me: "Jesus...and that harshness our ancestors learned from our oppressors."

Her: "Yup! You have to be perfect so you don't get the whip. You have to be perfect so they'll see you've assimilated and that will somehow stop them from viewing us as less than"

Her: "God that shit is so deep"

Me: "Yep."

Me: "And we never got praise from our oppressors. It was either no communication or negative consequences."

Her: "Truth. My nickname from my mom's side since I've been a kid literally means 'little fat girl' "

Her: "My mom told me she was only going to visit me...if I got into the doctoral program. Gracias, Madre"

Her: "This is her obligatory visit since I got in"

Me: "Ugh."

Me: "Being PoC sucks for your mental health."

Her: "But then we don't believe in mental health lol"

Her: "My mom HATES that I take an antidepressant"

Me: "Ugh. God."

## PIMPIN' MY PIGMENT

Today, I sat in a presentation about the college experience for black students. I listened to the presenters speak upon reasons why black students choose to attend college (or not) and why black enrollment in higher education is declining sharply with no end in sight.

The presenters went over theories as to why this phenomenon is occurring. They questioned us: "Is it the lack of diversity and inclusion initiatives? Is it because of the current political climate?" We grilled ourselves on the why and the how, and we began to brainstorm plans to increase black enrollment in higher education.

A black girl raised her hand. We turned and listened intently.

She spoke of her experience as an undergraduate student at a local institution. She talked about how, as a black woman getting a college degree at a predominantly-white university in a predominantly-white area, she knew she would be one of the only black folks on campus. Her expectations on diversity were extremely low.

But then, she said something that struck me.

"Since I'm one of the only black women at the college," she explained to us, "they suddenly want me to do everything. 'Hey, can you do this?' 'Hey, can you sing at this event?' 'Hey, do you wanna be in this brochure?' They out here tryna' pimp my pigment."

I sat back. *Pimp my pigment.*

I remember in undergrad being asked to have photos taken of me for my institution's website. They're still using my photos, years later; and I have long graduated from the university. It's a bit unsettling to see a photo of yourself on a university Facebook page and that photo is years old.

I remember in elementary school being taken from classroom to classroom by my music teacher, his hand on my shoulder. At the entrance of each room, he would say with excitement in his voice and sweat beading on his forehead, "Listen to her voice! This is amazing! Arielle, sing!" And I would sing, on command, to please him. He would clap. He asked me to be the lead cantor at church every Thursday. To this day, I still struggle to sing in front of people.

I remember in high school being pulled in to an administrative office. The white man sat behind his desk and cheerfully told me about how I could be the face of diversity at the school – me, a softspoken teenaged girl with a 4.0 who just so happened to be black.

"We'd love to have you at this event!"
"Would you be willing to have photos taken for us?"
"They're looking for a diverse representative, and I *immediately* thought of you!"
"We need someone to sing the national anthem at the basketball game. Can you do it?"

I never knew the feeling of, "Are they only asking me because I'm black?" had a name. The abuse of my melanin, the white man's use of my blackness, the tag of "token black woman" forced upon me by racist institutions has a name, a phrase, a nomenclature.

*Pimping my pigment.*

I did not ask for this, like how prey does not ask to be hunted upon by predators. I did not scream, "Hey! Use my blackness!" I did not give permission to view my melanin as a recruitment tool, as a "look at how diverse we are!". I did not give consent for people and institutions to appropriate my black girl magic, to bottle it up and sell it on the black (white?) market in recruitment brochures, in elementary school church choirs, and in high school administrative offices.

My black girl magic is not a commodity to sell, especially by white folks, to further their own diversity and inclusion agendas.

My pigment has been pimped.

But as of today, I refuse to work in the white folk's Red Light District any longer. I am taking back my melanin magic, and I will no longer work on these diversity and inclusion street corners hookin' for these white-ass fools.

My black girl magic is *mine*, and you ain't pimpin' my shit no more.

## THINGS TO NOT SAY TO YOUR BLACK FRIEND, LOVER, CO-WORKER, OR CLASSMATE

Your skin is so beautiful
My first time was with a black woman, you know
God, black girls are fucking hot

You're my African Queen
Give me all your black girl goodness
I can't wait to taste your black girl juices

Do you tan in the sun, or do you get lighter?
Can I touch your hair?
Are your nails real?

All lives matter
Blue lives matter
Just listen to the cops,
And you'll be fine

You're not like other black girls
You're smart, y'know?

You're not "ghetto"
I consider you white
You're one of us!

Racism is over,
Since we have a black president now
I'm not racist;
My best friend is black!

Are black people okay with...?
Is it true that all black people...?
Do black people like...?
(*I'm not a representative for all blacks, god damnit.*)

All white people have African ancestry
Blackface isn't that big of a deal
It's just a costume

You know you've made a black girl mad
When she's wagging her finger at you!

White privilege?
I worked hard to get where I am!
Show me this "white privilege";
I'd sure love to cash it in.

You know,
Vikings had dreads, too

I'm not racist, but...

At the end of the day,
We're all one race:
The human race.

## YOU CANNOT HAVE MY "BYE, FELICIA" WITHOUT MY "BLACK LIVES MATTER"

### A TEXT CONVERSATION

Me: "I'm sick of only seeing bars listed as LGBTQ hangouts"

Friend: "OOOOOH HOT FIRE"

Me: "And then going only to see white gay cis men who think it's okay to touch my hair and use AAVE and touch me inappropriately because ITS [sic] OKAY HONEY IM [sic] GAY AS FUCK YAAAAS"

Me: "And I'm just like please stop using the language if going to the west end of Louisville [Kentucky] scares you"

Me: "I hate these cafeteria white folx who see black culture and only appropriate the parts they think are cool"

Friend: "Bloop"

Me: "Who just go down the cafeteria line picking YAS QUEEN and BITCH SLAY while turning their noses up at black lives matter and rap and AAVE"

Friend: "Like if you ain't going past 12th street [in Louisville, KY] don't talk like you live there"

Me: "Quit picking the dessert table clean and eat some goddamn vegetables"

Friend: "OH MY GOD THAT'S [sic] A GOOD ONE"

Friend: "that [sic] changed my life"

Me: "You can't have my bye Felicia without my black lives matter"

Me: "No dessert without dinner boo"

# THE NINA, THE PINTA, AND THE SANTA MARIA

## TW: USAGE OF THE N-WORD

*I was inspired to write this piece after seeing a friend's photo on social media. She is a white, cis, able-bodied woman; and in the photo, she is hugging the mainmast of the Santa Maria. There she was, staring in to the camera lens, grinning from ear-to-ear, embracing an essential part of the ship that carried Christopher Columbus and his crew. While she seemed elated in the photo, I felt otherwise.*

How many enslaved people had traveled the seas
    Not on the deck or in the crow's nest
    Not as captains nor as first mates
    Not towards treasure or adventure?

Those people traveled
    In blackened holds
    Crammed shoulder to shoulder
    Below the deck
    And out of sight

The stench of piss
    And vomit
    And shit
    And decaying bodies
    The only sensations they know
    as they rock upon the mighty ocean


They traveled as victims
    As servants and laborers
    As cotton-pickers
    As "stupid niggers"
    As future white man's property


They traveled towards hell
    En route to torture
    To servitude and abuse
    To whips and chains
    And pain and racism


How many slaves had traveled the seas
    Torn from homes rich with culture
    And rife with tradition
    To be sold like cattle
    To Bland white men
    Too lazy to tend their own crops
    Or please their own wives?

Millions of slaves had traveled those seas
      And in the hull of my heart,
      I carry their pain and afflictions


My white-owned ancestors
      Tried to desperately claw their way
      Out of the ship's hold
      And I swear
      I can still feel the wood
      Under my fingernails


So when I see you hug
      That mainmast,
      I am shaken


Because while you take pride
      In the white man's first step
      In 1492,
      I think about my ancestors
      That were forced
      To sail the ocean blue

# OBSERVING THE WHITE CIS MAN

[*As I've gotten older, I've begun to observe people more and more. I'm constantly hyperaware of my surroundings – I am consistently watching and listening to my environment, observing human behaviors and looking over my shoulder. I'm not sure if this is a result of the lessons I've learned in life – that I should always be aware of my surroundings because I'm a woman and/or because I'm black – or a result of having Generalized Anxiety Disorder (GAD). But either way, I'm always observing; and I've discovered that white, cis, able-bodied men move through this world in a unique, entitled, privileged way. Below are just a few of my observations.*]

I am sitting in a coffee shop, laptop open, ready to write. I look up briefly to people-watch; and as soon as I look up, a woman of color steps in to the shop. She approaches the counter and begins to order. She is kind, and meek, and gentle, consistently saying, "yes, ma'am", "no, ma'am", and "please".

A white man walks in to the shop. He opens the door with force, the door flying open. He takes loud, large strides through the shop, his head up and chest out as he looks straight at the baristas behind the counter. He gives off a, "I deserve to be here" air, a, "you better serve me" attitude that only white men who are not aware of their privilege seem to have.

He steps up to the counter and leans on it, his eyes bouncing between the woman of color at the counter and the barista taking her order. He taps his credit card on the counter impatiently. He stands very close to the woman of color, invading her space, violating her privacy and autonomy. She rushes through the rest of her order, pays, and scurries away, obviously uncomfortable.

Once she leaves, he places both hands on the counter, leaning to talk to the barista. He invades her space as well. He bellows his order, not making eye contact with the barista. He does not say, "Thank you" or "yes, ma'am" or "no, ma'am"; he merely says his order, pays, and walks off.

---

I am walking through the mall. My city has three prominent malls, and this one is the most "affluent": it is located on the teaser side of the city, which is predominantly white and upper-middle class. You can tell that this mall is made for people with money (AKA, generational wealth); as I walk through it, I see Von Maur, the Apple Store (one of two located in my state), Anthropologie, Brooks Brothers, Kate Spade, Sephora, and many other stores my people have neither heard of nor could afford because we're too busy paying bills in a system that works against us. I make sure to hold my head high while I walk.

I play a game in my head. "How many black people will I see in this mall that *aren't* working for the mall?" I begin counting. It is a full twenty minutes before I see another black person who meets the criteria.

As I am playing my game, a young, white man begins walking towards me. He is with a group of friends, also white men. I suddenly change my game: "Will he move out of my way?" I smile to myself.

I look him right in the eye and continue walking. I have no plans to step aside for him; to say, "excuse me"; to look away. I match his body language – head up, chest out, strides long and purposeful. We get closer, and neither of us make any indication of stepping around the other.

We are mere inches from each other before I lose the game of "are you too entitled to move out of the way" chicken because God knows what this guy will do if I bump in to him. He turns his head to continue glaring at me as I step around him. His friends turn their heads to look at me as well.

I then remember that white, cis men can feel entitled to many things, including walkways and the space in them. "Make way for the king", I guess.

---

I walk in to my local gym. I take a quick glance around the workout area I use...all white men. They all glance at me as well. As soon as our eyes meet, I look away. I keep my chin up because I refuse to let their eyes make me look down. I can tell they are still glancing at me as they lift weights. I suppose a tattooed black woman with a shaved head and hairy legs and armpits is a strange sight.

As I wrap up the first half of my workout, I walk by an older, white, cis man, who is sitting on an exercise machine. He looks over his glasses at me, his bifocals sitting low on his nose. He watches me walk past him, his brow furrowed as he studies me. I hold my head high still, but I am tense because I remember that the white folks who fought vehemently against desegregation, proudly sipped water from "whites only" water fountains, and called my ancestors "niggers" with the hard -er are my grandparents' age; those mindsets do not go away overnight. Once I'm out of his field of vision, I shoot him a sideways glare. I think to myself, "This one's for my grandparents, and their parents, and their parents, asshole."

I am walking through a parking lot to my vehicle. In my field of vision, I see a white, cis man walking with his two young, white children. He is gripping the youngest one's wrist very tightly and marching him through the parking lot; the child's hand is red from his father's relentless grip. His brow is furrowed. The youngest child struggles to keep up, stumbling through the parking lot as his father drags him by his tiny wrist. The older child follows closely and quickly behind, skipping and laughing. "Why are white men inherently violent, even to their own children?" I think to myself. I am worried for the children because I know that abuse is a cycle.

I am sitting at another local coffee shop, writing this book. I am typing away on my computer, and I overhear a conversation between a white, cis man and his female friend.

"I hear what you're saying. I just think you're wrong."

I glance over. He is sitting back, his legs spread wide in is seat and his arms crossed. He lifts his eyebrow towards his friend. She is sitting with her legs crossed, taking up as little space as possible. She sits silently.

As he starts explaining his argument, I go back to writing. I can hear the aggression in his voice, and I can see out of the corner of my eye that he is leaning forward in to the woman's space. She is leaning back now, listening.

Sometimes, white men even feel entitled to suppress others in an aggressive way. I am no longer surprised at this behavior.

———

At the end of each day, I wonder how white, cis men can so unabashedly take up space, invade comfort zones, and move through the world as if it belongs to them. As a black, queer, femme, polyamorous, neurodivergent woman, I cannot even wrap my head around the concept.

But then I remember: the world was made for them, not me. "All hail the king", I guess.

# I AM A(N) _____ BLACK WOMAN

I go to the coffee stand at my workplace.

The black woman behind the counter greets me loudly.

"How you doin', baby?" She shouts from behind the counter.

I wave and respond with, "I'm good, honey; how are you?"

She grins and replies, "I'm good!"

As I walk away, I yell for her to have a great day.

She waves and yells, "You, too, baby!"

I am a loud black woman.


I stumble across an article online while mindlessly scrolling through social media.

"Oklahoma sorority sister booted after posting blackface video".

I read the news article.

It details a white sorority sister who posted herself in blackface on a social media outlet.

She did this the day before Martin Luther King Day.

I roll my eyes and let out a frustrated sigh.
I am an angry black woman.


I meet with a group of women for a drink and a night out.
We are all black and queer.
We revel in the comradery.
We laugh over drinks and the absurdity of the current political climate.
Later, in a nearby nightclub, we drink more.
We dance, flirt, and kiss one another in the dim lights of the nightclub.
I am a sexual black woman.


A friend, also a black woman, rests her head on my shoulder.
I rub her thigh while she confides in me that she is tired.
She is tired of racism, of sexism, of struggling so hard to live and just exist in this oppressive world.
I tell her that it is okay to be tired, that I am here for her, and to care for herself above all else.
I am a nurturing black woman.


I crawl in to bed after a long day.
I had therapy today, where I had to unpack decades of generational oppression while also coming face-to-face with the difficulty of living as a black, queer, polyamorous, neurodivergent woman.
I sigh in to my pillow.
My energy for the day is gone.

I am an exhausted black woman.


I read another news headline.

"White man accused of killing Black shopper pleads not guilty to federal hate crime charges."

He went to a Kroger in my city, in broad daylight, and shot two black people.

They died from the gunshots.

I think about if I had been in that Kroger that day.

Would I be dead, too?

I also think about how these racist people live among us.

I am a terrified black woman.


I go to a local conference that focuses on supporting diversity.

The conference is filled with people of color.

I fill my cup with wholesome conversations, general comradery, and hugs and pats on the back.

"Stay strong out there, sis," a black woman says to me in passing.

I wave to her and say, "You, too, honey."

We smile at each other with teeth, the exhaustion of existence in our eyes.

We are supportive black women.


I schedule a lunch with the other black women in my department at work.

I become more excited as we finalize times.

The emails being exchanged are full of smiling emojis, exclamation marks, and enthusiastic responses.

I'm looking forward to being surrounded by amazing, hard-working, beautiful black women.

I am a happy black woman.


While I am sometimes loud,
    Or angry,
    Or sexual,
    Or nurturing,
    Or exhausted,
    Or terrified,
    Or terrified,
    Or happy,
    I always have
    And always will be
    A black woman.

# BLACK COMFORT

(I *found out that a co-worker and close friend passed away unexpectedly. I was at a loss; I couldn't comprehend his death, his sudden "gone-ness", and the fact that I would never see him again. I cried all night and had nightmares, but I dragged myself to work the next day.*

*I went to the coffee shop at my workplace to get a coffee, which is what I do almost every day. I put on a fake smile – fake it 'til you make it – and asked for my coffee. The barista, a black woman, handed me a coffee cup and said, "Have a great day, baby." I pulled out my card, and she shook her head. Again, she said, "Have a great day, baby"; and she flashed me a big grin.*

*The free coffee meant more to me than the barista will ever know. This passage is for her.)*

Black comfort is
Feeling your mother pull your scalp as she braids your hair
And you tell her about the little girls
Who made fun of your plaits
And colorful barrettes
That clacked together when you ran across the playground
Away from their laughing and pointing
And your mother huffs through her nose and says,
"Don't worry 'bout them, baby;
They ain't shit"


Black comfort is
Your father
Kissing you on the cheek
When he is normally a stern, distant man
With wrinkles on his forehead
Because his brows are always furrowed
You are shaken, shocked, speechless
When one day, he says in his gruff voice,
"I'm so proud of you"


Black comfort is
Family holidays
Plates overflowing with food made with heart and soul
Collard greens, mac n' cheese,
And down-home, quality time with family
Your auntie laughs with a mouth full of chitlins
And your heart has never been fuller

Black comfort is
    Mutual anger
    Between you and your sisters
    Because Becky done said somethin' out the side of her
neck again
    "You know, we're all one race...the human race"
    You side-eye your homegirl and say,
    "Can you believe this bitch?"
    With no words spoken


Black comfort is
    Chatting about
    4C hair
    Ashy niggas
    Bitches who ain't shit
    And what products we use
    To keep our skin clear
    And melanin glowing


Black comfort is
    Free vanilla hazelnut coffee
    From the black barista
    With a big grin
    And a gold tooth


Black comfort is
    That same black barista
    Looking directly in to your eyes and saying,
    "Have a great day, baby"

Black comfort is
    Mutual existence
    Mutual struggle
    and mutual triumph
    In the face of death

## THINGS I HAVE BEEN CALLED
## THROUGHOUT MY LIFE

Arielle
    Ari
    Sis
    Sistaberry
    Sissy
    Leo the King


Black
    Afican-American
    Nigger
    Black bitch
    Bitch
    Cotton-picker
    Slave


Sexual awakening
    African Queen
    Chocolate drop

45

Nubian princess
Black girl goodness
"My first black girl"
Exotic


Daddy
    Papi
    Mistress
    Ma'am
    Baby
    Babygirl


A gift
    A blessing
    Friend
    Lover
    Best friend
    Soulmate
    Future wife


Abusive
    Toxic
    Mentally ill
    Depressed
    Anxious
    PTSD sufferer
    Disabled
    Migraine sufferer

Daughter
 Sister
 Auntie
 Cousin
 Mother (of a cat; don't get it twisted)


Author
 Writer
 Presenter
 Speaker
 Keynote speaker


Owner
 Founder
 Entrepreneur


Powerful
 Strong
 Brave
 Role model
 Hero
 A revolution

# DON'T FUCKING TOUCH MY HAIR

Would you go to the Louvre
    And put your hands
    All over Mona Lisa?


Would you travel to Florence
    And violate the Statue of David
    With your grimy, unclean hands?


Would you trek to New York City
    And smear your fingerprints
    On Starry Night?


If you wouldn't put your hands
    On these works of art
    Then why the fuck is it okay
    For you to touch the art
    That I have on my head?

This set took hours
    These braids took time
    This weave took ages
    These curls took spans
    And believe me
    It doesn't need
    Your fucking hands


It's a simple concept, really:
    Don't touch priceless works of art
    But since you struggle to grasp this concept
    Let me sing a song for you,
    To the tune of the ABCs


A, B, C, D, E, F, G
    Keep your fucking
    Hands off me
    You can't touch
    This hot set
    Lest you get
    Fucking wrecked
    A, B, C, D, E, F, G
    You can't touch this bomb 4C


You know to not touch me
    Please no flash photography

# 23ANDME RESULTS

## AND AN ANALYSIS THEREOF

Results

**Arielle Clark – 100%**


Sub-Saharan African – 55.4%
   *Nigerian – 19.3%*
   *Ghanaian, Liberian, & Sierra Leonean – 12.8%*
   *Senegambian & Guinean -6.3%*
   *Congolese – 2.5%*
   *Southern East African – 0.1%*
   *African Hunter-Gatherer – 0.1%*
   *Broadly West African – 10.0%*
   *Broadly Congolese & Southern East African – 0.8%*
   *Broadly Sub-Saharan African – 3.6%*


East Asian & Native American – 30.3%
   *Filipino & Austronesian – 28.3%*
   *Native American – 0.7%*
   *Broadly Chinese & Southeast Asian – 1.0%*

*Broadly Northern Asian & Native American – 0.1%*
*Broadly East Asian & Native American – 0.1%*

European – 13.3%
*British & Irish – 2.0%*
*Scandinavian – 1.0%*
*French & German – 0.8%*
*Broadly Northwestern European – 5.8%*
*Broadly Southern European – 1.2%*
*Broadly European – 2.5%*

South Asian – 0.3%
*Broadly South Asian – 0.3%*

Unassigned – 0.7%

Analysis
**Arielle Clark – 100%**

Sub-Saharan African – 55.4%
*Ancestral Struggle – 19.3%*
*Melanin Magic – 12.8%*
*Black Pride -6.3%*
*Unique Hair Patterns – 2.5%*
*Full, Pouty Lips – 0.1%*
*Smack Ya' Mama Food – 0.1%*
*Shared Experiences – 10.0%*

Strength Through Adversity – 0.8%

Tongue-Suckin', Finger-Snapping Attitude and Self-Love – 3.6%

East Asian & Native American – 30.3%
Rice with Every Meal – 28.3%
Listening to Grandmommy Speak Tagalog on the Phone – 0.7%
High Cheekbones – 1.0%
Humility – 0.1%
Looking Much Younger Than I Actually Am – 0.1%

European – 13.3%
Invasion – 2.0%
I Didn't Ask for White Ancestors – 1.0%
Christopher Columbus, the Terrorist – 0.8%
"They are Savages; We Can Make Them Better" – 5.8%
All Lives Matter – 1.2%
"The Police are Here to Protect Us" – 2.5%

South Asian – 0.3%
My History is Lost to Colonialism – 0.3%

Unassigned – 0.7%

# MY FRIEND'S BABY

## A CONVERSATION

*(A white friend of mine who is a woman recently had a baby. I met him for the first time when he was 7 months old.)*

Me: *Cooing at the baby, who is giggling and smiling.* "Hi, baby! You're so cute! Hi, sweetie!"

Friend: "He's a smiley boy."

Me: "...wait." *Turns to look at my friend.* "...Has he ever seen a black person before?"

Friend: "Yes! ...wait. ...Yeah! ...wait. Now I have to think..."

Me: *Stares at her in silence.*

Friend: "...wait. Yes. ...yeah! I'm pretty sure."

Me: *keeps staring.*

Friend: "He doesn't get out of the house a lot! My mom won't even let me put him in daycare."

Me: "Why?"

Friend: "Measles!"

Me: "Ah. ...so has he ever met an LGBTQ person before?"

Friend: "...now that one I have to think about."

Me: *Stares at her again.*

Friend: "I think so...yeah. Yeah!"

(*My friend left with her baby after that. As I watched her leave, I thought to myself, "...wait. Has that baby ever met a black, LGBTQ person before? ...well, he has now."*)

# HOW TO SUPERVISE A BLACK WORKER WHEN YOU'RE A WHITE BOSS

## A QUICK LIST

1. Yes, I am black. Acknowledge it. Let's not ignore the elephant in the room here.

2. Yes, my blackness will affect how I see you, just like how my blackness will affect how you see me. Admit it...again, let's not ignore the elephant in the room here. You're judging me subconsciously because of my skin color. And as a result, I judge you because you're white and judgmental.

3. Stop saying, "I understand". No, you don't. You're not black. When I tell you about something race-related that is bothering me (e.g., "these white men keep staring at me because they don't think I belong here"), don't say, "I understand". You don't. Period.

4. Stop talking over me.

5. Stop interrupting me.

6. Do *not* "supervisor-splain" me. That is, don't talk over me in a meeting (or any conversation, really) to explain something *I just said.* Fuck hierarchy; I know my shit.

7. I am not below you. I am your equal. You just have a different title. So stop treating me as a "lesser". You know who else got treated as "lesser"? My enslaved ancestors. Fuck you.

8. I have resting bitch face because I have to deal with white folks all day saying shit out of the side of their necks. So yes, if I look irritated, I probably am because some white colleague probably said something like, "Man, they're working me like a slave today!" It's not personal. But it actually is. Either way, watch what you say.

9. Analyze your language. See "Man, they're working me like a slave today!" above. Shit ain't cute, or funny, or clever. It's just alienating. That also trivializes my ancestors' experiences.

10. Don't say dumb shit. For examples of dumb shit, read chapter 7 of this book.

11. Don't. Fucking. Touch. My. Hair. See chapter 15.


12. If all else fails, or if you're unsure, follow these rules:
    a. Don't.
    b. No.
    c. Stop.
    d. Be quiet.
    e. Yes, that's offensive.
    f. Watch your privilege.

# A SUPPORTIVE FRIEND

## A FACEBOOK CONVERSATION

*(I was struggling with depression and having suicidal thoughts. I was frustrated with my body for constantly being sick, and I felt like I didn't belong anywhere because of my multiple identities. I felt alone, helpless, and hopeless. A friend reached out via Facebook.)*

Her: "Maybe I'm a stranger and this is weird. Maybe this means something. I hope it will...your post hit me today. It resonated deeply...

Her: "I'm not here to say it's easy or gets better or anything on a motivational poster or social movement"

Her: "Just to say you're not alone"

Her: "And I feel you"

Me: "Thank you. Greatly appreciated."

Her: "You're an incredible person so far as I can see. [...] powerfully vulnerable, compassionate, intense, and beautifully fluid"

Her: "Hope all the ppl [sic] in your life holdup [sic] a mirror to you for you to see you through their eyes!"

Me: "You're really sweet."

Her: "Thanks .. mean it tho [sic]. Your [sic] humanity is tangible and powerful and RARE"

Me: "It doesn't feel like it, haha. Just feeling a little weak. And meaningless."

Her: "Yeah ... and that's real. And your [sic] honoring it. Sitting with it. Letting it be that until it isn't that again. And that's what's so powerful ... you allow yourself to be human"

Her: "...we dare to be real, which makes us more individual.....there aren't 1000000 ppl [sic] out there who like what we like or think what we think or do what we do or are 'like us' cuz [sic] we're being genuine"

# TOO BIG FOR BOXES

I have been shoved in to boxes all of my life

Crammed in to trunks and coffins
  Of different shapes and sizes
  To please people whose crates
  Were too small for my big, loud, black existence

I have been jammed in to tiny portmanteaus
  And it is reminiscent of how
  My ancestors were packed to the brim
  In the bottoms of slave ships

They were shoulder to shoulder
  Chest to chest
  Atom to atom
  In those tiny, seedy slaveship underbellies

I think of them and their discomfort
    When white people tell me
    How to dress
    How to talk
    How to walk
    How to eat
    How to live


My ancestors were crammed in to
    The dark and dank recesses of those ships


And their descendant is crammed in to
    The sunless and sticky cavities
    Of the boxes white men create for me


They try to shove square pegs into round holes
    And white ideals down black women's throats


But like my great great great great grandparents
    Who would rather leap in to the unforgiving ocean
    And get swallowed by the merciless waves
    Than be shoved in to a white man's ship
    I would rather tear the casket open
    Until my fingernails bleed
    Than be stifled ever again

I have been shoved in to boxes all of my life
    And I will fight to the very end
    Because I refuse to let whiteness
    Swallow my blackness


And I refuse to let a box
    Define whom I am
    Especially since that box was not made
    For the likes of me

## I SLEPT WITH A BLACK, QUEER WOMAN WITH LOCS AND ASKED HER AN IMPORTANT QUESTION

Me: "What's your type?"

Her: "Black."

# TEDXBELLARMINEU

## BREAKING THE CHAINS THAT BIND: LEARNING TO LOVE MY BLACKNESS

*(I gave a TEDx talk at Bellarmine University of February 28th, 2020. This chapter is a transcript of my talk.)*

**Introduction**

Hi. My name is Arielle Clark. My pronouns are she, her, hers. I am a 27-year-old Louisville native – born here, raised here, have never left, and won't leave for a while; since I've started my own business here (more on that later).

Growing up in Louisville, I went through the typical trials and tribulations – finding friends, navigating the horrible world of puberty, having crushes, and being a rebellious teen. My experience was greatly influenced by my identities – I am a queer, neurodivergent woman (which means that I am LGBTQ+ and have mental illness). But most importantly, and most obviously, I was influenced by my race. In case you didn't notice, I'm black – shocking, I know! While people can't see my queerness or my neurodivergence, people can see my race. And that greatly influenced how I grew up.

My name is Arielle Clark. I am black. And I hated it.

## Body of Presentation

"I am an amalgamation of mothers -- the result of millions of contractions, of thousands of cervixes dilating, opening wide, singing, chanting, yelling arias of new life on the West African plain.

I am the product of hundreds of black wombs carrying black babies with ten black fingers and ten black toes and one black struggle. And while our mothers carried us, little did we know that the kicks and jostles we gave our mothers' swollen, stretch-marked stomachs were merely practice for when our black feet would touch the ground and carry the weight of slavery and womanhood.

We began to train our legs before we knew what they were, so that we could run to our sisters for comfort while running for offices and running from our overbearing mothers who are just trying to protect us from the harsh, harsh world.

The blood in my veins is that of Audre, of Maya, of Diana and Halle, of Afro-queens and 4C braids and plump, pursed lips and wideset hips.

I am the descendant of soulful sisters, of slaves who ran and activists who spoke.

My history is rich, like my ancestors weren't, who made a dollar out of 15 cents and cuisine out of inedible scraps our slaveowners threw to us, deeming us unworthy of good meat and unrestricted freedom.

This is my history. Black is my blood, and rich is the African soil from whence I came to be."

I was born black. I have always been black. I will always be black. I cannot separate myself from my blackness physically. However, growing up, I wanted desperately to separate myself from my blackness. I wanted to somehow step out of my skin. I wanted to be white so badly because from my birth, I was told what "whiteness is better" actively and passively. The moment I was birthed, I was exposed to the vehement hate of blackness. I hated myself. I hated other black people.

My anti-blackness started in my childhood. With colorful barrettes clacking in my hair, I remember non-black children asking if my hair were real. When speaking up for myself, or reciting things in class, both children and adults commented on how articulate I was. But their compliments dripped with inherent racism – I wasn't articulate because I knew big words and had an upper-level vocabulary; rather, I was articulate because I didn't speak the way that my fellow black people spoke.

There's something called African American Vernacular English, or "AAVE". AAVE is the modification of the English language that is rooted in the American South and Southern African English. Growing up with an immigrant grandmother from the Philippines, pronouncing English words precisely was essential. Further, the neighborhood in which I grew (as well as the schools I attended) were majority white, so I was not exposed to AAVE until a later age. Because of my lack of AAVE, white people applauded my speech and vernacular. At that time, I was proud.

But you know what? The reason that white people applauded my English was because they inherently saw AAVE as a lack of understanding of modern English. AAVE was black laziness in understanding and speaking English, which is rooted in racial stereotypes regarding black people. Back then, I saw myself as sophisticated. Now, I see myself as separated from my own black ancestors.

That was just the beginning of a long stream of racism and internalized self-hate.

As I grew through my teens, it got worse. High school was, by far, the worst. While I cannot give you a play-by-play of everything that occurred, here's a snapshot:

A student asks me, "Is your hair fake? Is that weave?" Everyone laughs. I laugh along with them because my hair is real. I'm not one of those black people.

I am walking down the hallway. Another student yells, "What are you doing out of the cotton field? Get back to work!" They laugh. I laugh along with them because I'm educated. White people like me. I'm not one of those black people.

A friend sees me before class. They jokingly hold their hand sideways, motioning that they're holding a gun. "Look! I'm black!" They laugh. I laugh along with them because I'm in school and not dealing drugs. I'm not a thug. I'm not one of those black people.

"Uh oh! Arielle's mad! We're gonna get shot!" My friends laugh. I laugh along with them because I'm sophisticated. I can handle conflict in a non-violent way. I'm not one of those black people.

"You know," a friend says as we're walking together, "I like you. You're not like other black people. You're not ghetto or anything. You see, there's African-Americans, there's black people, and there's n-ggers. You're African American. You know how to act." I grin with pride. I am one of those black people. Well, I am African-American.

Turns out that the reason my "friend" liked me so much was because of my proximity to whiteness and my growing distance from black culture. Blackness made her uncomfortable. Blackness was bad to her. And blackness was bad to me, too. I looked down on other black people. The closer they were to black culture, the more I disliked them. I turned my nose up at black people who were immersed in black culture. But that's all I knew: to deny black culture, to see it as bad. I grew up steeped in anti-blackness. I knew nothing else.

In my 20s, I took a philosophy class during my undergraduate studies. One of the required readings was Audre Lorde's Sister Outsider. There was an essay in the book that discussed, in detail, how black women internalize racism and sexism from which they suffer the moment they are born. Black women internalize this hate and release it on other black women, judging others using the criteria by which they are judged by white society. After reading that essay and digesting it, I realized that I, too, had internalized all the pain and criticism I had experienced. I was lashing out at my own people – my family – due to my own pain.

And that was when my journey to self-love began. I began

the long, arduous, beautiful process of unlearning over 20 years of anti-blackness. And like a flower, an African cape daisy, I bloomed beautifully in to my own black self-love.

I read more Audre Lorde. She opened my eyes even more as I read more chapters of more of her books. As a black, queer woman, Audre speaks to my soul.

I made more black friends. This happened in stages. At first, I only befriended black people "like me" -- spoke "like a white person", did not wear fake hair, and looked down on other black people. Then, I started interacting with black people that I was taught to fear and dislike. I then began to realize that the fear and dislike I was experiencing was a result of racist rhetoric fed to me for over two decades. I realize that black existence -- AAVE, ornate wigs and hair-styles, loud laughter, and soul food -- is a rich culture all its own, not an absence of sophistication.

I began to critique why I feared and disliked certain black people in the first place. I research white privilege, white supremacy, the history of slavery, the history of the inunda-tion of white ideals on black people. I realized that every-thing I learned about black people for the last two decades is because white people are inherently racist. I felt shocked and betrayed. These people who had praised me for being so "sophisticated" all my life were actually against me accepting my blackness. I vowed to never turn my back to my own people again.

I moved in with a black roommate at the age of 25. She taught me how to do my hair and how to care for it properly. At first, I found myself going back to my old ways -- critiquing her loudness, criticizing her hairstyles, and wondering why she spoke the way she did. I caught myself and dismissed my racist past.

I dated my first black person at the age of 27. I didn't realize how much more deeply I could connect to a black partner than a white partner. I could, with confidence, speak about "Black Lives Matter", how exhausting code switching is, and how I know so little about my own race and culture as a result of how I was raised.

I drove to the West End of town, all the way to 22nd Street. I felt myself become afraid as black people watched my car go by. Would I get shot? Robbed? Kidnapped? I exited my car and held my purse close. When I realized how tightly I was clutching my bag, I released my grip. I looked around and realized, "These are my people. I was raised in fear of them and in fear of myself. Why am I afraid?" I smiled and relaxed. I smelled delicious food in the air. Multiple black women complimented by hair and outfit, calling me "baby" and "sweetie". Black men tipped their hats at me. I realized that I am home there.

I give talks around the city, the state, and the region

regarding my blackness. I speak proudly about my race, and I teach people to love and accept black culture and existence. I challenge people to unpack their racism and privilege. I face the challenge head-on.

And now, I own a business – a black, queer business. I am the owner and founder of Sis Got Tea, Louisville, KY's, first black-owned, LGBTQ-owned, woman-owned tea café.

**Conclusion**

Loving myself has been one of the most difficult journeys of my life. I remember when I was a teenager that I wrote about a crush of mine commenting on how beautiful her crush's skin was. Her crush's skin was white. I wrote about how her skin was porcelain, moonlight, powdery snow. I wrote about how my skin is dark, like tar, like coal, like dirt. But now I describe my skin was mahogany, black, deep, and rich. It tells stories of rich culture and resilient ancestors.

I hated myself until my mid-20s. But I'm not mad at myself for it because I've come to realize the following: Assimilation is survival. Self-love is a revolution.

My name is Arielle Clark, and I am black. And I don't hate it anymore. I love it.

## COMMON NORMALIZED BEHAVIORS
## THAT ARE ACTUALLY TRAUMA
## RESPONSES

Hitting your children
Punishing your children
when they disagree with you
Not telling your children "good job"
Only reacting to your children
when they do something bad
Only giving negative or neutral reactions,
not positive ones, to your children
Working until you drop dead

Skin bleaching
Colorism
Worshipping of light-skin
"Good hair"

Judging other black folks for being too ghetto, too
    ratchet, too hood
Thinking that being educated makes you better
Believing there's a difference between African-
    American, black, and nigger

Hating your skin
Hating yourself
Hating your people

# CAN I DEPEND ON THE MEDICAL SYSTEM?

(*I went to a local allergy doctor to get a skin test for food allergies. Apparently, there's a difference between sensitivities and full-on food allergies. I knew I had allergies or something of the sort; multiple foods would give me a range of reactions, from gastrointestinal distress to itchy gums. I wanted a comprehensive review of what I'm allergic to, and my experience was...interesting.*)

The nurse leans over me from behind, studying my back. I am hunched over on the stool. I can feel my skin itching and pulsing. I can't scratch, and it's driving me crazy.

She stares at my back for a bit, and she stands upright. "Well, no notable reactions. Looks like you don't have food allergies! You had a very light reaction to almonds, peanuts, soy, and clams." I hear her shuffling some papers around. "Food allergies show as bumps on the skin, while sensitivities show as redness around the injection site. No redness. Just a few tiny bumps!"

I perk up slightly.

*Something isn't right*, I think to myself. *I react to so many more things. Peanuts, yeah, okay. Almonds, yeah, those make my mouth itch and my stomach hurt. Clams? No fucking idea; I never eat those. They freak me out.*

*What about apples? Pears? Peaches? Celery? Carrots? Cherries? Pomegranate? They all make my mouth itch. I start sneezing. My ears begin to itch. My stomach begins to turn. There's got to be redness. There must be. I've gotta be sensitive to more things. Is this all in my head? Have I been imagining my reactions?*

Out of fear of challenging the doctor, I nod and say, "Okay, sounds good." Damn my conflict avoidance. Although, she is a nurse. She studied these things. I should trust her, right?

She leans over me again and squints. "Hm, for some reason, the histamine isn't reacting. Let me grab someone." Her tennis shoes slap the floor as she walks out. My back still itches.

She comes back with a black nurse, who smiles at me. I try to occupy myself with random thoughts to distract myself from the itching.

"Oh, there's redness." I hear the black nurse say. The first nurse, a white woman, leans in.

"Oh, I see it now!"

I am sent off with my results and a paper explaining oral allergy syndrome, an allergic reaction that occurs due to cross-reactivity between plant proteins from pollens and fruits. Surprise: my allergy to birch is so bad that I can possibly cross-react with the following foods:

- Apples
- Peaches
- Plums
- Pears
- Cherries
- Apricots
- Almonds
- Carrots
- Celery
- Parsley
- Caraway
- Fennel
- Coriander
- Aniseed
- Soybean

- Peanuts
- Hazelnuts


I stare at the paper in my car. I begin to think again.


*What if that black nurse hadn't been around? I would have gotten the wrong answer. They would have sent me on my way. I would have gotten incorrect information about my allergies.*


*Why couldn't the white nurse see the redness at first? It's because of my skin color, isn't it? God, if a simple allergy test on black skin had results that were overlooked, where else has the medical system failed us black folks?*


I think about all the black folks in my life and how the medical system has failed them.


A family member suffers from GI problems. She goes to doctor after doctor, specialist after specialist. She has not gotten any answers, and years have passed. She is still suffering.


I go to the emergency room at 4 AM one night. For days, my chest has been tight, my left arm has been tingling, my chest has been physically hurting, and I have felt a sense of impending doom. The nurses and doctor view my chart and see that I have a history of panic attacks. I spend over 4 hours explaining to them that no, this is not a panic attack; I know exactly what my panic attacks feel like and how long they last. This is no panic attack. After being brushed off, the doctor shrugs at me. He does not have an answer. I am sent home. The chest pain and shortness of breath last for almost a full month. I still don't know what happened. All the symptoms I had are symptoms of a heart attack.

I talk with a friend who is fat. She mentions pain that she is having in her legs. She mentions quietly, "The doctor just keeps telling me to lose weight." She explains that they never ask her about anything else. They always just brush her off and say, "You need to lose weight."

A friend casually tells me about the birth of their daughter. They mention that they had a terrible birthing experience and have trauma because of it. They briefly describe pursuing legal action against the hospital, but they decide to end the pursuit; it became too expensive, too laborious, and too time-consuming.

I stumble across an article during the summer about Lyme Disease after going on a hike with friends. The article mentions that one of the symptoms of Lyme Disease is a large, red rash with a target-like appearance. There is a photo of a black man with the Lyme Disease rash on his back. Because of the darkness of his skin, the rash is barely noticeable to the untrained eye. I think to myself, *How many black folks have Lyme Disease and don't know it because the doctor didn't look hard enough?*

The night after my allergy test, I lie in bed, staring at the ceiling. My back still itches a bit. The itch reminds me of my visit.

"Oh, there's redness." The black nurse says.
    "Oh, I see it now!" The white nurse says.

It sets in that the medical system has failed so many black people. My mind wanders more.

*How many black folks are misdiagnosed? Not diagnosed at all? Sent to doctor after doctor for no reason, shuffled around and around until they're too tired and too broke to keep searching for answers? How many black folks have died because of our flawed medical system? How many black folks are suffering right now? This system is fucked. It's so fucked. We're fucked. God damnit.*

I can feel myself begin to cry because for the first time, I question if I, or any black folks, can fully depend on the medical system.

# HAVE ALL OF ME OR NONE OF ME

Stop fucking splitting me
　　Like dry lips in bitter winter
　　Cracking, bleeding, hurting,
　　And sore


Stop picking and choosing
　　The parts of me to love
　　Stop pulling my limbs off my body
　　The tearing skin and dislocating joints
　　Make me scream at a volume
　　That can shatter glass
　　And my exhausted, already-broken heart


You want my black but not my queer
　　My queer but not my black
　　My polyamory but not my black
　　My black but not my polyamory
　　My queer but not my polyamory

My polyamory but not my queer
And on
And on
And on


I am a whole fucking person
    And my identities are intertwined
    Like a tight braid against my scalp
    Like vines on a tree
    Like the fingers of lovers
    Locked together forever


You cannot separate me
    You would have to work hair by hair
    Vine by vine
    Finger by finger
    Atom by atom


And by the time you would finish
    Would fingertips would be raw
    Red
    Bloody
    Destroyed
    And I would already be gone
    Your blood staining my braids,
    My vines,
    And my fingertips
    Off to find a lover
    Who won't waste their time

Or mine
Trying to complete the impossible task
Of loving only a piece of me


I am whole
    A full person
    With identities that combine
    To make a beautiful being


I am black
    *And* polyamorous
    *And* queer
    There's no *or*
    Or *except*
    Or *sometimes*


Have all of me or none of me
    Because you cannot have part of me
    Without having all of me


Stop fucking splitting me
    I am whole
    I am complete
    And I am a fucking package

## TO BE POLYAMOROUS

This black love is sacred
Abundant
Priceless
All-encompassing
And most importantly
Infinite

I cannot love only one at a time
For if I tried,
They would drown in the ocean of my romance,
The holy water of my affection
Filling their overwhelmed lungs
The taste of my never-ending passion
Rushing along their taste buds
So quickly and forcefully
That it burns on the way down

They would drown in my depth
My passion
My emotion

My fervor
My pussy
My arms
My all

I love so uniquely
And each partner is like a fingerprint
Our love swirling, creating patterns and pictures
On our swelling hearts and heaving chests
And I can identify each partner
By their prints on my aorta
Each one rare
Particular
Individual
Beautiful
Incomparable
Perfect

I cannot stifle this copious passion
If I tried, my cheeks would swell
And swell
And swell
Until the skin broke
And my lips would be forced open
And like a dam breaking

All my love would flood the streets
Neighborhoods
Towns
Cities
Nations
The entire fucking world

I am polyamorous
Because my love is immeasurable
Like the horizon over the ocean
The sand at the beach
The number of kisses I've given
The "I love you"s I've said

My polyamory is beautiful
My love, boundless
And I will love this way
Kiss this way
Fuck this way
Forever
Just like how long my love
Will flow
And exist
And flourish

# TO OUR YOUNGER BLACK SELVES

Dear black younger self,
Don't put that relaxer in your hair
You'll fry your ends
And the scabs from the chemical burns
Will itch like hell
And besides,
Your natural hair is beautiful

Dear black younger self,
Don't take too much Aleve
When your tightly-wound braids
Give you headaches
Aleve irritates your stomach,
And you'll be nauseous for days

Dear black younger self,
You will receive the following questions
Throughout your entire life:
"Do you tan in the sun or get lighter?"
"Can I touch your hair?"

"Are your nails real?"
At first, smile and respond
After being asked the 14th time,
Ignore them completely
And on the 15<sup>th</sup> time,
Let that motherfucker know
That that shit don't fly

Dear black younger self,
Colorism is real
Don't forget that dark-skinned folks
Have it much harder than light-skinned folks
And that light-skinned folks are favored
Always remember humility
And check your privilege

Dear black younger self,
Whether trans,
Or non-binary,
Or gender-non-conforming,
Or agender,

All are welcome in the family
And if any family says otherwise
Then they ain't family no more
And their black card?
REVOKED.

Dear black younger self,
Hold your head high
When you walk through white crowds
Because they'd love to see you fall
Your existence is a revolution

Dear black younger self,
You are a shining star
A glimmering diamond
Despite being told
Over and over
And you are nothing
But dark skinned
And lesser than

Dear black younger self,
Roll your neck
Pop your tongue
Snap your fingers
You're making music with your body
And communicating in a language
That is beautiful, complex, and our own

Dear black younger self,
I see you
And hear you
And feel you
And know you
And I love you so deeply

Dear black younger self,
You are fearfully made
And wonderfully created
To change the world
One step at a time

Dear black younger self,
It is okay to cry

You don't have to be strong
All the time

Dear black younger self,
Unclench your jaw,
Relax your shoulders,
And release the stresses
Of racism and sexism
From your muscles

Dear black younger self,
I see the load you carry
You are not alone
Your ancestors are carrying the load with you
For we are all in this together

Dear black younger self,
You are an uprising
A rebellion
And a revolution

Dear black younger self,
I hope this book gave you comfort
And laughs
And a-ha moments
Because I wrote this for you
To show you
That you are not alone

Dear black younger self,
Here's a book
For your shelf

# ABOUT THE AUTHOR

Arielle Clark – she, her, hers – is stumbling through life as a black, queer, neurodivergent (post-traumatic stress disorder, major depressive disorder, and generalized anxiety disorder, thank you very much), polyamorous woman in her upper 20s. Born and raised in Louisville, Kentucky, she is currently trying to find her life's purpose while simultaneously prepping for her 30s.

Arielle Clark currently spends her time taking the zodiac way too seriously (she's a Leo and is, of course, very dramatic), owning Sis Got Tea and playing around with tea way too much, and trying to remember to take vitamins and drink water on a semi-regular basis. She is currently based in Louisville, Kentucky, with her son, an 18-pound cat named Alfonso whom she would die for. Her favorite coffee shop is Highland Coffee, which served as her informal headquarters while writing this book.

www.ingramcontent.com/pod-product-compliance
Lightning Source LLC
Chambersburg PA
CBHW051431090426

42737CB00014B/2926